AF270601

ARIZONA CARDINALS

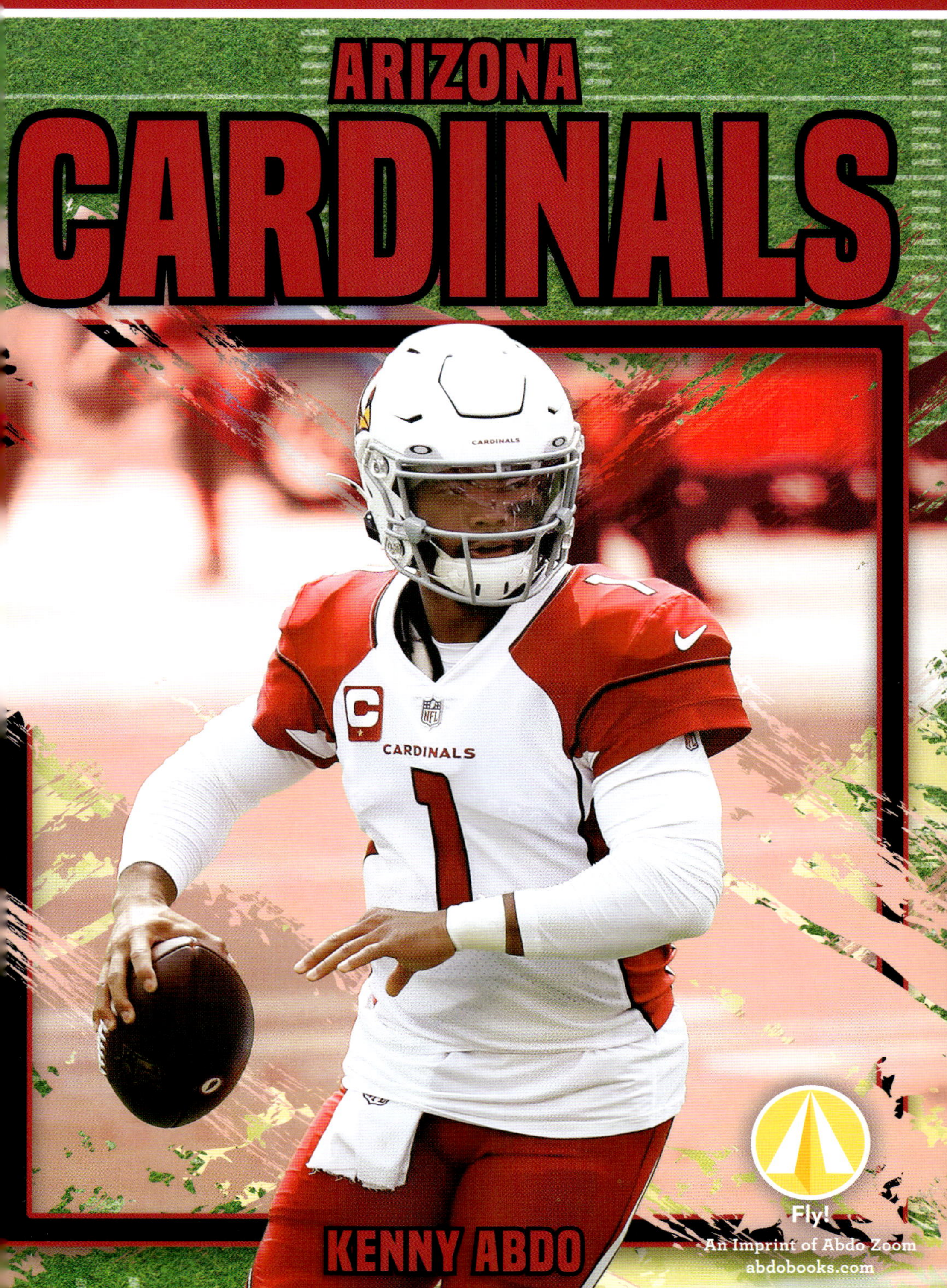

KENNY ABDO

abdobooks.com

Published by Abdo Zoom, a division of ABDO, P.O. Box 398166, Minneapolis, Minnesota 55439. Copyright © 2022 by Abdo Consulting Group, Inc. International copyrights reserved in all countries. No part of this book may be reproduced in any form without written permission from the publisher. Fly!™ is a trademark and logo of Abdo Zoom.

Printed in China.
052021
092021

Photo Credits: AP Images, Getty Images, Icon Sportswire, iStock, Newscom, Shutterstock PREMIER
Production Contributors: Kenny Abdo, Jennie Forsberg, Grace Hansen
Design Contributors: Candice Keimig, Neil Klinepier

Library of Congress Control Number: 2020919466

Publisher's Cataloging-in-Publication Data

Names: Abdo, Kenny, author.
Title: Arizona Cardinals / by Kenny Abdo
Description: Minneapolis, Minnesota : Abdo Zoom, 2022 | Series: NFL teams |
    Includes online resources and index.
Identifiers: ISBN 9781098224516 (lib. bdg.) | ISBN 9781098225452 (ebook) |
    ISBN 9781098225926 (Read-to-Me ebook)
Subjects: LCSH: Arizona Cardinals (Football team)--Juvenile literature. | National
    Football League--Juvenile literature. | Football teams--Juvenile literature. |
    American football--Juvenile literature. | Professional sports--Juvenile literature.
Classification: DDC 796.33264--dc23

TABLE OF CONTENTS

ARIZONA CARDINALS

Flying high since 1898, the Arizona Cardinals are the oldest football team in the United States.

From multiple playoff visits to reaching the **Super Bowl**, fans known as the Red Sea love watching the Cardinals "protect the nest."

KICK OFF

The Cardinals were founded in 1898 by businessman Chris O'Brien. He bought used jerseys from the University of Chicago. The jerseys were faded, so the color was called cardinal red.

9

The Cardinals won their first **championship** in 1925. They struggled through the 1930s and 1940s.

But in 1947, the Cardinals were the
NFL champions. The team won the
Western Division title in 1948.

In 1960, the Cardinals moved from Chicago to Saint Louis. They won their division in 1974 and 1975. But they lost the playoffs both times. In 1988, the Cardinals made another move. This time to sunny Arizona.

TEAM RECAPS

The Cardinals won seven games in their first season in Arizona, but did not make it to the playoffs. In 1998, **quarterback** Jake Plummer led the team to nine wins. The team won its first playoff game in 51 years!

In 2003, **rookie** Anquan Boldin made NFL history in his debut game. He gained 217 receiving yards, the most by any receiver in their first NFL game!

The Cardinals played the Pittsburgh Steelers at **Super Bowl** XLIII. They lost 27–23. The Cardinals made it to the playoffs again in 2014 and 2015. They lost both times to the Carolina Panthers.

The Cardinals finished the 2019 season with a 5-10-1 record. **Quarterback** Kyler Murray played his first game against the Lions. He had two touchdowns, an **interception**, and had 308 passing yards for an incredible debut.

Linebacker Chandler Jones racked up 19 **sacks**, eight forced fumbles, and placed second in 2019's Defensive Player of the Year Award. In week five of 2020, Jones suffered a season-ending injury in his right biceps.

CARDINALS
WVB
CARDINALS
55

HALL OF FAME

Aeneas Williams became a Cardinal in 1991. He led the **league** in **interceptions** in 1994 with 9 and fumble return yards in 2000 with 104. He retired with 55 interceptions for 807 yards. Williams was **inducted** into the Pro Football Hall of Fame in 2014.

Larry Fitzgerald has been a Pro Bowl pick 11 times. He was named the 2008 Pro Bowl **MVP**. Fitzgerald holds the team record for the most receptions in a single season. He leads the team with more than 17,000 receiving yards, 1,400 receptions, and 120 touchdowns.

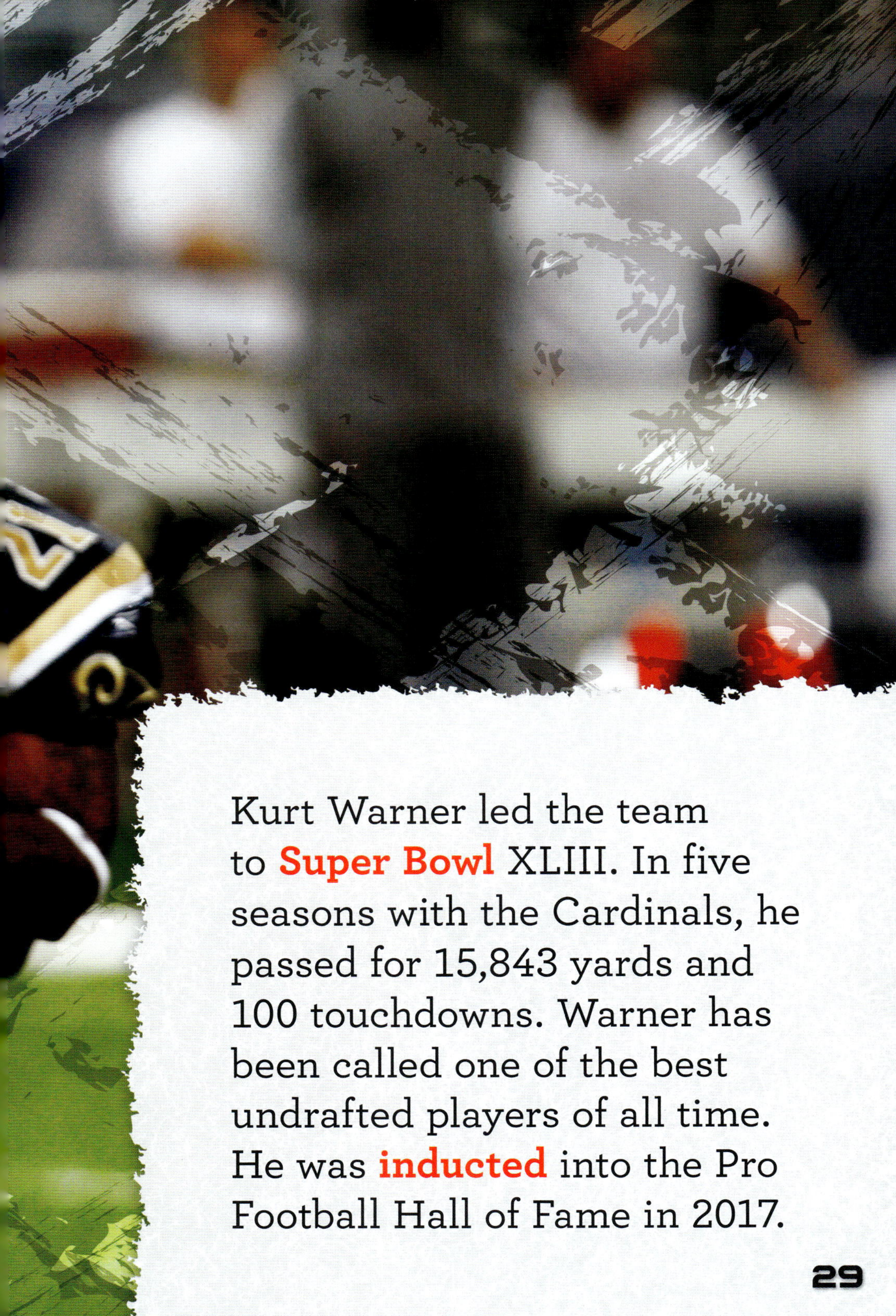

Kurt Warner led the team to **Super Bowl** XLIII. In five seasons with the Cardinals, he passed for 15,843 yards and 100 touchdowns. Warner has been called one of the best undrafted players of all time. He was **inducted** into the Pro Football Hall of Fame in 2017.

GLOSSARY

championship – a game held to find a first-place winner.

induct – to admit someone as a member of an organization.

interception – when a player catches a pass that was meant for the other team's player.

league – a group of teams that compete against each other.

MVP – short for "most valuable player," an award given in sports to a player who has performed the best in a game or series.

quarterback (QB) – the player on the offensive team that directs teammates in their play.

rookie – a first-year player in a professional sport.

sack – when a quarterback is tackled behind the line of scrimmage while still in possession of the ball.

Super Bowl – the NFL championship game, played once a year.

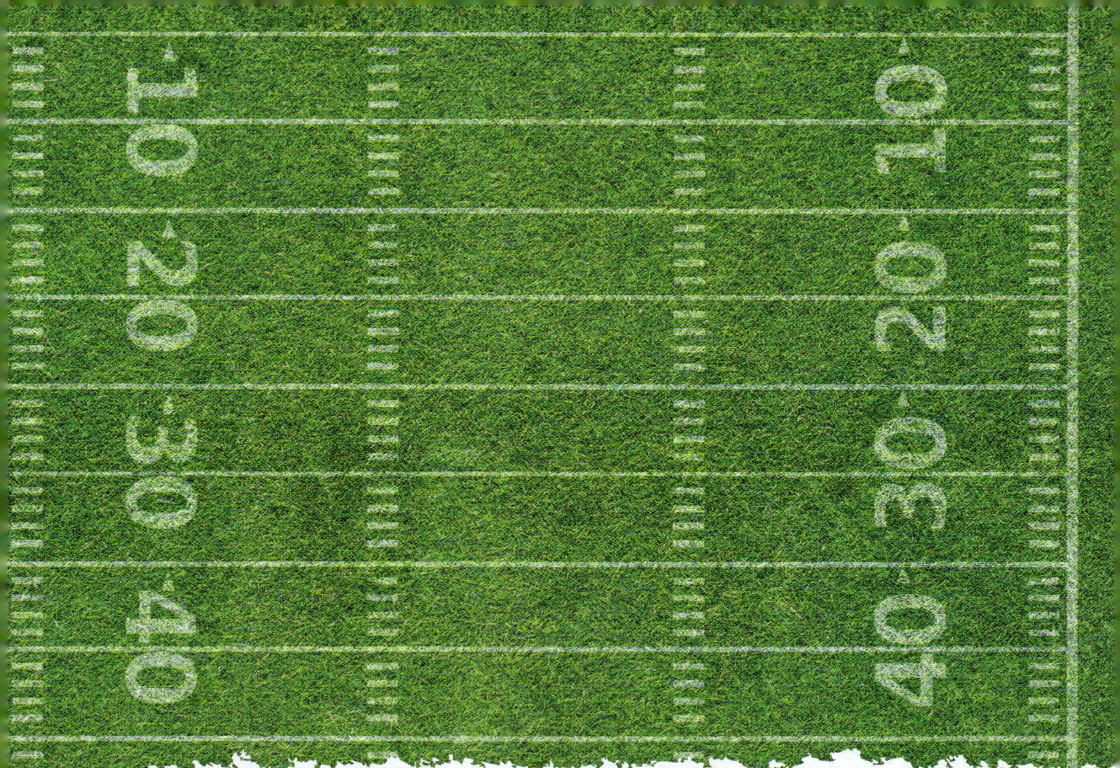

ONLINE RESOURCES

To learn more about the Arizona Cardinals, please visit abdobooklinks.com or scan this QR code. These links are routinely monitored and updated to provide the most current information available.

INDEX